My Antarctica

Aug 2022

Dear Joan,
your teaching in the
classroom and through
your poems continues
to guide me. I
am so lucky
to know you.
Thank you,
Janlori

poems by

Janlori Goldman

Finishing Line Press
Georgetown, Kentucky

My Antarctica

Dedicated to my brothers,
Michael and David

ACKNOWLEDGMENTS

Gratitude to the following publications:

Rhino, "Candy," (2022)
American Journal of Poetry, "Where Should the Birds Fly After the Last Sky?" (2020)
The Stillwater Review, "On the Day She Left" (2020)
The Cortland Review, "Anna and Pincus in the Black Sea, 1913" (2019) and, "At the
Corner of 110th Street and Broadway" (2010)
Beloit Poetry Journal, "The Feeders are Empty, Empty for Days" (2019, as "An Old
Hunger")
Oberon Poetry Magazine, "Nearing Sixty" (2019)

With deep appreciation for Marilyn Nelson's *A Wreath for Emmett Till*, and Joan
Larkin's "Blackout Sonnets," both of which guided and held me through the writing
of *Renovation*.

A community of writers sustains me—thank you to Cris Beam, Laure-Anne
Bosselaar, Peter Covino, Lori Desrosiers, Elisabeth Frost, David Groff, Christian
Gullette, Suzanne Hoover, Joan Houlihan, Robin Messing, Alicia Ostriker, Sarah
Van Arsdale, and to those who are gone, especially Barbara Hammer, Kamilah Aisha
Moon, and Jean Valentine. I brim with gratitude for Karen Dodds, una curandera
estupenda y mi cuñada. Always love for my daughter, Maya Rose, for her courage,
strength, and dedication to healing our world. And for Katherine, my first reader and
sweetheart extraordinaire.

Special thanks to Leah Maines for choosing my manuscript, and to Christen Kincaid
and the editorial staff at Finishing Line Press for making it a book.

Publisher: Leah Huete de Maines
Editor: Christen Kincaid
Cover Art: The Journey by Kristin Flynn
Author Photo: Maya Rose Goldman
Cover Design: Oxygen Design Group, Sherry Williams

Order online: www.finishinglinepress.com
also available on amazon.com

Author inquiries and mail orders:
Finishing Line Press
PO Box 1626
Georgetown, Kentucky 40324
USA

Table of Contents

One

Two

Three

One

*When you return from the country of Refusal,
what will you think of us?*

Katha Pollitt, from "To An Antarctic Traveller"

Candy

At night I want what will last. Lights out
      I reach under the bed for the can
            of *Charms* sourballs, pop the top,

sort the colors from least liked
      to favorite, end on cherry red—
            such syrupy sweet before drift.

With each piece I ease to being held
      by the mattress. The sucker's slow dissolve
            joins the body's settling sounds,

its gurgles and hums, like a car
      come to rest after a long ride, its chassis' groan,
            the hiss and sigh of an engine cooling—

those rough planets rolling against the roof
      of my mouth, all the next day my tongue
            runs along the raw spot, the hurt

I come to expect with any sweetness.
      The taste of bed. The taste of red.

My Antarctica

What might it take to be worthy,
        to be such a hero? Here I am, this lesbian

obsessed with a continent men ache
        to conquer, their conquest and strandings on ice

heralded as *heroic*. I want to stand
        on the south pole where all four directions

point north. All for the impossible hurrah
        of planting a stick on the earth's bottom,

an amazon's flag flapping in the wind.
        Sprout a scraggle beard that freezes with snot

and tears, lose a fingertip to frostbite, get lost
        and walk in snowdrift circles. Trudge across

a frozen desert for one thousand two hundred miles,
        eight months of food strapped to my back.

Mapmaker

Sometimes I get lost,
can't figure out where I'm going.
I try to make a map,

chart my own geography,
how the body rises up
and away from itself,

but the line between rock
and water seems impossible
to draw—even as this glacier

calves and sinks into
swallowing waves, leaving the
mother-side exposed to sky,

sipping air and gulping ocean,
sun on one cheek,
saltwater on the other—

I can split, be my own
fork in the road, lichen
growing over its gash,

or be the border wall
that guides my hand
as it moves in the night.

In these halting lines
I think, what use is a map anyway—
can't the right road

get us just as lost?

On the Day She Left

A hawk flies over the yard, blocks
        the sun, snatches a squirrel
                from the base of an ash tree.

Talons in her scruff, the mother is midair—
        her youngsters circle the trunk,
                search the sky, the small brood

confused by such exit—
        three siblings left to fend.
                With greasy hair and soiled paws,

they wait for her return.
        Wait to unlearn
                that a child can be left

by force—by the pull
        something stronger.

The Feeders are Empty, Empty for Days

I should replenish but I wait,
        see how many times the birds return

to a hollow bowl. Finches seek thistle,
        cardinals crave sunflowers—

are they looking for me, will they be glad
        when I arrive? The rabble nominates

the titmouse to cling to the tube, scrounge
        at the holes, glance at me with hopeful tuft.

Like the way we huddled on the floor
        at her bedroom door, children

with morning rumble. We sent in her favorite—
        in the dark he approached the bed,

stood near her head—*mom, lunch money?*
        He'd wait, see the pulled shades,

the bottle of scotch, smell her sleep.
        In the hall he divvied up three quarters,

three dimes. Coins tucked in our pockets,
        we walked to school, each making our way.

There's the titmouse, still clinging.
        I lumber out to the shed for seed,

vow to be better, to nourish what relies on me
        to feed our hunger.

Passover

Seders at the long oval table, all of us gathered in best clothes,
        Aunt Bertha's bulging blue dress, the strained buttons

on Uncle Joe's pressed shirt. We kids squirm and fuss, naughty
        with olives and celery sticks, crawling under the table

to tie Arline's right shoe to Irving's left. When it's time to open
        the door and welcome Elijah, we eye the breeze

moving toward the empty seat, the rattle and slurp
        of the stranger's wine cup, the shadow of his hungry face—

only then can we call for more matzoh balls in the broth.
        We eat and eat. Uncle Joe pushes back to undo his belt,

make space for a second helping of brisket. In that ritual and chew,
        the bickering doesn't know where to land—though our car

will be full of it on the way home. Those seders, a respite
        talk of our more recent exodus. But this year

we all seem lost, wandering again—now we are the Elijahs,
        searching for our table, for one open door.

Two

Renovation

1.

My house needs work so I let men in—
      each morning, with keys I give them, the men

push through, sure of their right to enter,
      to tromp the stairs in mud-crusted boots.

They hammer and clomp, break down
      sturdy walls, lug clumps of stuff to the curb.

Their hard-hatted infantry trembles oak planks,
      shakes loose decades of thick paint.

I shut a door, one they have not yet ripped out,
      think I can stay on my side with them on the other.

Under the door, choking grit creeps in, settles—
      at night I scrub the scarred floor.

When I speak, the men begrudge
      a fleeting civility, grins slipping—

2.

Begrudging a fleeting civility, their grins slip to
           sneers in the instant before they turn away

when I ask for what I need to feel clean—
           don't smoke in my house, please wipe

your shoes—and there it is, side-eyed
           disdain, a lopsided lip twitch

that says, *I could take you right now, rip*
           your clothes off, stupid cunt. I can see

the original tunnel from which these men broke
           into air, the look back at their mother's torn gape—

their thumbs hooked there still. How they smirk
           with the belief that where they came from

will always belong to them—*mine, mine, that's*
           mine—as they reclaim that first house.

3.

The door to my first house—all mine as firstborn,
      the only child carried in or out for three years.

Frosted panes bookend the door, a body blurred
      on the other side. A staircase leads to my crib—

face pressed against the bars, I use early words—
      out! me out!—but no one comes to lift me.

I pull myself up and over, cling to the crib's ribs
      as I shimmy to the floor. Mother wants me

contained, at a distance. She keeps me in a high-walled
      playpen, the next cage I scale. There's this photo,

me chubby with grimace in the pen, arms stretched up in plea,
      like a Jacob on her ladder, or Blake's defiant child—

rung by ascending rung away from the earth,
      arms lifted into the sky of escape.

4.

My arms lift to the sky of escape, but there is
    no way out from under the dirt

of his body—my legs, impacted roots,
    strain to break the surface, away from

the only air in that shack—his breath
    acrid with cigarettes and beer—

no rungs to climb, no door unlocked—
    that day I lose all sense

of being twelve —become no age,
    not even my name stays,

I am a body held under, a body
    for touching—I struggle

to remember, did I resist or lift
    into those hands?

5.

Did I lift into those hands, did I like the feel of hungry
      eyes on me—to be the thing that feeds

a hunger? Weekends, dad wants me in his car,
      his cover for escapes to other women's homes,

where I wait with Nancy Drew until he emerges,
      ready to go. He never asks, but I know

not to tell, how much must never be told,
      that certain stories wear a gag, celluloid

silent on their reels. I know when to open,
      what to conceal—what he wants, what it takes

to keep him close. On the return, he buys me soft-serve
      at Carvel, swirled into a sugarcone. At its full height

it spirals to a tip and bends over—like a child,
      neck dipped to her chest, submissive, pliant.

6.

The swan's neck dips to her breast—submissive, pliant—
        as the movie begins. The 2nd grade teacher

shuts the blinds, flips on the projector, a hot light
        with two reels, the top one full of story empties into

the one below—the click of metal wheels turning,
        a tight tunnel of light. In the beam

flimsy shirts of dust particles cling
        to air, float inside the radiating shaft,

a lit stream flows through the room.
        I see the fabric,

feel atoms enter and leave my body,
        how the air carries itself—chin up—

despite tattered clothes. The world opens to reveal
        what's always there but not seen with the light on.

7.

What is always there but not seen with the light on—
    that dark swan on the screen, paddling towards a

huddle of white swans. Rumps waggle under
    the surface as the dark swan is pecked

by a pale swaggerer—others join in,
    beaks battering the drenched midnight of her feathers.

Spurned, her yellow eyes bulge with shock as she tries
    to swim into the circle. The clan attacks—*out! out!*

She searches for a sheltering wing—*mother, don't you*
    remember how you warmed me under your belly, how I

paddled behind you even when the others lagged? Mottled
    with spit, she watches them drift away.

An empty reel clacks in the florescent classroom. Dozens of eyes
    see me, head bent, snotty and scruffed, gulping sorrow.

8.

Head bent, I look in the toilet at the pulp of ripening fruit,
      a rambutan in water, not the salty amnio it knew as home.

A moment ago in the bookstore, pain's butting beak, a sticky trickle
      between my legs—I lock the restroom door, feel how it leaves

my body, hear the weight of it hit—what might have been
      my son, my daughter. How could I not know I was pregnant?

True, I was late, but never imagined my body could hold another life.
      I fumble to recall the sex—it must have happened.

Do I scoop it in my palm, lift it from this bowl for proper burial,
      like how I cradled broken-necked birds that hit the window,

buried them still-warm—how could I do less for my own failed life?
      What if Membrane still beat, if I held her like the bluejay?

But I can't claim the no-name that dropped from me.
      Callous womb, refusing what's yours. I flush.

9.

How callous of me, Charlotte, refusing to leave
     your body undisturbed. At the hospital the doctor

stops me at your door—*kidney failure, nothing to do
     but wait.* You lie there, nearing the other side,

breath sucked through a gurgled straw.
     For hours I speak to your closing face,

hold your hand, your ring cinched
     in swelling. *Does it hurt?* I ask.

Say, *don't go.* In that limbo
     you can't see or speak.

A nurse offers morphine, turns it up.
     When I ask for your ring, the mortician breaks

a sweat—says, *it won't be easy.* Why does he
     say that, what rage burns in him?

10.

A rage burns in him, blazes through the basement,
        our playroom. He takes up a toy tomahawk,

axes the youngest child first—always the last
        to hide—as we older two crouch behind the dryer—

baby brother screams as dad hisses, *why must you insist?*
        No god grabs that Abraham by the wrist to spare

our Isaac. Spent for now, emptied of whatever fatwood
        fuels his flame, he drops the weapon,

shuffles upstairs. Nancy Sinatra on the record player
        singing about boots made for walking,

how that's just what they'll do, *one of these days*
        these boots are gonna walk all over you.

A child beaten grows up with a missing
        limb, a limp in the brain.

11.

With a limp in the brain, I build a box
  to lock away films: the clip of his arm

striking, the scene with a kick from her pointed
  slipper, a small person pinned. That attic box

stays shut—but the reels turn all the same,
  the projector's light trapped under

a lead lid. Lopsided, I bump into walls,
  misstep off the curb, walk off-kilter.

What upends the child's body rattles
  the growing brain—a crouch under the desk,

inside the closet waiting for an icepick
  to crack me out of a freeze. The way I opened

my legs, averted my face. Attic and basement—
  bookending what accumulated in that house.

12.

What accumulated in that house—a very bad dog,
  skulking in a corner, sniffing about for a nibble

after the lights go out, nuzzling myself
  when I can't break free from sleep.

What remains in the morning—
  a scruffy cur that needs to be fed,

like our childhood dog who tracked the scent
  of hot chocolate packets dad hoarded,

pockets jammed with them after a motel stay—
  that retriever ravaged the Swiss Miss, tore

through her blond braids and aproned skirt, inhaled
  foil with the mix. Drooled powder coated

the shag rug, then buckets of shit—such a sick pup—dad
  drubbed the dog, who flinched at a raised hand.

13.

The bugs flinch at my raised hand, like any
        creature afraid to be squelched. I let them in,

left the door open when I woke up to pee.
        The bedroom—I forgot to protect it,

so distracted by going into the hall
        to get to the bathroom. Why didn't I spring

for a nicer hotel? Mosquitos smell their chance—
        everywhere I go, those buzzers hunt me,

suck my blood, raise an itchy welt.
        Fruitless, my clap and swat routine,

until I remember that night in Turkey,
        drunk on Raki, dancing on the bed

in my underwear, snapping a towel
        against the walls. I smashed those fuckers.

14.

Thought I'd smashed the bad dog, kept her muzzled and caged,
        swapped her for a tough pup strutting on bulked-up haunches.

But during the renovation, the motley box of exiles—dark swan,
        girl with limp, cowering cur—explodes. A black hole sucks us

into its maw, seals the exit from our windowless cell.
        I can't make my house safe. The structure I built

needs work but no one said taking it down to the studs
        means blasting it to smithereens, unable to make out

precipice from steppe. I asked for it, gave up the keys—
        they track in gutter muck, deconstruct the armor.

When the locks refuse my key, the past growls up
        to meet the present. I may hurt someone. I may not

survive. The beloved, she is frightened. I don't see it
        coming. My house needed work. I let men in.

15.

The house needs work so I let men in—
        they manage a fleeting civility, then let it slip.
                They enter the door to my house, once all mine.

Arms lift to the sky of escape, but there is no exit.
        Do I lift into their hands, like the feel of their hunger—
                a swan who lays head on breast, submissive?

What is always there but not seen: head bent
        to my chest, gulping sorrow, ashamed of
                this callous body, refusing to honor what's hers.

Such rage burns in men, their fire sweeps through my basement.
        With a missing limb, a limp in the brain, I build a box to hold
                what accumulates—lock away creatures

that flinch at a raised hand. I thought I'd smashed my bad dog down,
        but she's chewed through her muzzle. We're starting to bark.

Three

Vandal

In the shack a chipped plate waits
     in the corner, hungers to hold

        something urgent in its shallow palm—
           a coat's button with thread still attached,

        a broken key. That shack opens
           its door, creaks with longing

for a scrounger to dust off its secrets,
     break the vined silence,

        recover a rubbed dish anxious for a spoon,
        for a desperate tongue—

Where Should the Birds Fly After the Last Sky?

Mahmoud Darwish, 1941-2008

On the road to Nablus I think of you,
　　　　your wrecked heart blooming

on rocky hills, a horse's shadow alone
　　　　in a field. Anemones spread

in resolute red—in warning or welcome
　　　　it's too early to say.

A candy store pocked with bullet holes
　　　　churns with cement mixers,

makeshift machines coating almonds
　　　　in sweet liquid. The shopkeeper says,

taste this after all you see. In a season
　　　　of unripe things, I bite into green almonds,

taxi to the mountain top to watch the village
　　　　long in the valley. Gusts of pigeons

blow against stone—all I have been taught
　　　　smacks against the rockface.

As a child in synagogue I fit a quarter
　　　　into a cardboard slot to *plant a tree*

in Israel, millions of coins
　　　　now tangled roots reaching

for each other in the subterranean world
　　　　that knows nothing of walls.

Anna and Pincus in the Black Sea, 1913

Anna Akhmatova, 1889-1966

Anna plunges into the ocean in thin dress,
      swims for hours, her friends on the jetty perturbed
            in corsets and rubber boots—she emerges, salt-stiff,

an ancient shell. My grandfather Pincus swam that same Black Sea,
      boasted of his muscle and distance, of reaching a far shore
            with stamina enough to make it back—

see how he chased Anna into the sea? A furtive rendezvous
      beyond sight of friends on the shore—
            a respite from the ripening terror.

During the revolution Pincus and his young bride Miriam
      snuck out of Russia. Anna remained,
            named those deserters traitors, memorized poems

before setting them on the stove's flame. In her winter room
      lush with lemon tree, the citrus blooms as Anna writes,
            making dozens of promises it can't keep.

A few branches might snap, but profuse fruit
      toughen its limbs, prepares it to bear stress
            in seasons ahead. She considers relieving the weight

with a twist at the nub of attachment,
      though there's ripeness to consider. How can she know
            when it is about to be too much, how to decide

which to nip early so the rest can survive?

At the Corner of 110th and Broadway

They wear blue latex gloves, the people in blue uniform.
    Six cops. That's what it takes to subdue one woman,
        limping with a rotten hip, pork chops in her blouse—

a swoop of police in flashing cars to handcuff one.
    Six cops. That's what it takes to subdue one woman,
        confused about the fuss, so many people watching and lights,

a swoop of police in flashing cars to handcuff one
    lady with a gray pony tail. She asks an officer, *which door?*
        Confused about the fuss, so many people watching, and lights

blinding her to the stockboy who sees her stuff her blouse.
    The lady with gray ponytail asks an officer, *which door?*
        A stockboy calls, decides her hunger requires force,

one muddled grocery-boy sees her stuff her blouse
    at the moment his stomach rumbles. Surrounded by food
        he calls, decides her hunger requires force.

They wear blue gloves, come in blue uniform
    the moment her stomach rumbles, surrounded by food,
        limping with a rotten hip, pork chops in her blouse.

She remembers her boy at home, the day he was born, led to life
    by blue latex gloves, by people in blue uniform.

Nearing Sixty

for Alicia Ostriker

Chilly and damp, I take a slower walk across the yard,
        shovel mulch into the wheelbarrow—the rickety

contraption hees and haws as we make our way bed
        to bed, limn shredded bark under roses and trees.

Knees to dirt, palms pat the earth and I hum, *that's it,*
        there you go. But death is here in April's nascence.

Just as my body prepared for childbirth—hips spread
        and bones softened to gasp open—

this season the body stiffens to a more narrow purpose,
        where brutal pruning of new growth

doubles June's blooms, where last year's sapling
        that didn't survive its first winter

molders in the compost bin. This spring is different,
        not just the creak and halt of yard chores,

but I see that what dies back may not return,
        see I am now too old to die young.

Love Poem for Ernest Shackleton

British explorer who led the first Trans-Antarctic Expedition, 1914

To be such a hero, to be so worthy—Sir Ernest,
      you let whip in the wind all hope

of a first crossing. Captain, in woolen mitts
      and scratchy undies, ice split the ship,

the cracking and sinking, your crew stranded.
      Hollow with hunger, you trudged

on blackened feet, your only aim to save the men.
      And the dogs—rugged huskies—you ate them.

Seals and gulls too. As for Mrs. Chippy,
      stowaway cat, you shot him—

knew you couldn't feed or eat him.
      At each calamity you took the right turn,

paddled a wooden boat across a gale-tossed ocean.
      On frost-bitten nights you conjured a lover—

O my Shackleton, how you growled into her neck—
      whisky, berries, buttered toast—

entered hungry and hard, made her come like an orange,
      sweet dream of juice. In the end

you stepped through to a blazing fire and close shave.
      Scraggled hull of a man, see why I love you?

Least of all for your conqueror's will,
      but for how you huddled your brothers,

all twenty-seven of them, rowed them home.

Janlori Goldman's first full-length book *Bread from a Stranger's Oven* (2017) was chosen by Laure-Anne Bosselaar for the White Pine Press Poetry Prize.

In 2013, her chapbook *Akhmatova's Egg* was published by Toadlily Press, and Gerald Stern chose her poem "At the Cubbyhole Bar" for the 2012 Raynes Poetry Prize. Her poetry has been published in *The Cortland Review, Rattle, Beloit Poetry Journal, Connotation Press, Calyx, Gertrude, Mudlark, Oberon Poetry Magazine, The Sow's Ear, Contrary, Naugatuck River Review, The Stillwater Review, WORDPEACE,* and *Rhino. Split This Rock* featured her poem "Ode to Jacob Blinder" as Poem-of-the Week in 2021.

Goldman is a founding co-editor (with Cheryl Boyce-Taylor and Yesenia Montilla) of *The Wide Shore: A Journal of Global Women's Poetry*, www.thewideshore.org, and worked with Paris Press on the publication of Virginia Woolf's "On Being Ill" paired with a long essay by Woolf's mother.

For many years Goldman worked as a civil liberties lawyer in Washington, D.C.. She teaches law, literature, and social justice, and is a writing mentor at Memorial Sloan Kettering Cancer Center. She lives in Accord, New York.

CPSIA information can be obtained
at www.ICGtesting.com
Printed in the USA
BVHW041134220722
642330BV00003B/198